Made in the USA
Middletown, DE
08 May 2021

39306724R00066